D0746305

Parakeets

Kelley MacAulay & Bobbie Kalman

🌴 Crabtree Publishing Company
www.crabtreebooks.com

Parakeets

A Bobbie Kalman Book

Dedicated by Leonora Van Egmond
With much love to Dan, Sarah and Katelyn, who are the songbirds of my heart

Editor-in-Chief
Bobbie Kalman

Writing team
Kelley MacAulay
Bobbie Kalman

Editors
Molly Aloian
Amanda Bishop
Kristina Lundblad
Reagan Miller
Kathryn Smithyman

Art director
Robert MacGregor

Design
Margaret Amy Reiach

Production coordinator
Katherine Kantor

Photo research
Crystal Foxton

Consultant
Dr. Michael A. Dutton, DVM, DABVP
Exotic and Bird Clinic of New Hampshire
www.ExoticAndBirdClinic.com

Special thanks to
Keith Makubuya, Sarah Chan, Lori Chan, Zachary
Murphy, Candice Murphy, Maria-João Figueiredo and
Parsley, Mike Cipryk, and PETLAND

Photographs
Marc Crabtree: title page, pages 3, 5, 6, 7, 12, 13, 16-17,
    18 (boy), 20, 22, 23 (boy), 25 (top), 28, 29, 30, 31
Robert MacGregor: pages 14 (all except parakeet), 15,
    18 (food piles), 19 (top), 21 (bathhouse)
Maria-João Figueiredo: pages 14 (parakeet), 18 (parakeet
    with treat), 21 (all except bathhouse), 23 (parakeet),
    24, 25 (middle and bottom)
Other images by Comstock, Digital Stock, Image Club
Graphics, and Photodisc

Illustrations
All illustrations by Margaret Amy Reiach

Crabtree Publishing Company

www.crabtreebooks.com   1-800-387-7650

Copyright © **2005 CRABTREE PUBLISHING COMPANY**.
All rights reserved. No part of this publication may be
reproduced, stored in a retrieval system or be transmitted in
any form or by any means, electronic, mechanical, photocopying,
recording, or otherwise, without the prior written permission
of Crabtree Publishing Company. In Canada: We acknowledge the
financial support of the Government of Canada through the Book
Publishing Industry Development Program (BPIDP) for our
publishing activities.

Cataloging-in-Publication Data
MacAulay, Kelley.
  Parakeets / Kelley MacAulay & Bobbie Kalman.
    p. cm. -- (Pet care series)
  Includes index.
  ISBN 0-7787-1757-7 (RLB) -- ISBN 0-7787-1789-5 (pbk.)
  1. Budgerigar--Juvenile literature. I. Kalman, Bobbie. II. Title.
III. Pet care.
  SF473.B8M279 2005
  636.6'864--dc22
                                                    2004011478
                                                    LC

**Published in
the United States**
PMB16A
350 Fifth Ave.
Suite 3308
New York, NY
10118

**Published
in Canada**
616 Welland Ave.,
St. Catharines, Ontario
Canada
L2M 5V6

**Published in the
United Kingdom**
73 Lime Walk
Headington
Oxford
OX3 7AD
United Kingdom

**Published
in Australia**
386 Mt. Alexander Rd.,
Ascot Vale (Melbourne)
VIC 3032

Contents

What are parakeets?

Parakeets are birds. A bird has a beak, two legs, and wings. A bird has feathers to help it fly and to keep it warm. A bird's tail helps it steer when the bird is flying. There are many types of parakeets. The parakeets shown in this book are often called **shell parakeets**. In many countries, shell parakeets are known as **budgies**. Parakeets are part of a group of birds called **psittacines**.

A parakeet's body

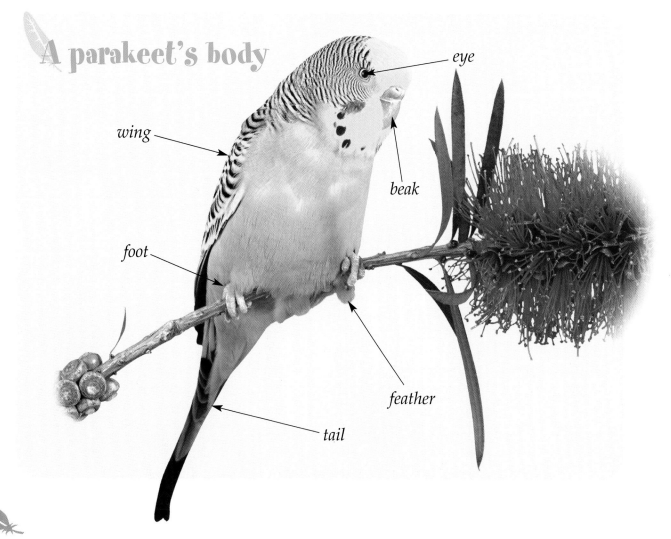

eye

wing

beak

foot

feather

tail

4

Wild relatives

Pet parakeets are related to **wild parakeets**. Wild parakeets are not tame. They live in the **grasslands** of central Australia. Groups of wild parakeets live in trees. They sleep in different trees every night. Most wild parakeets are green and yellow. Pet parakeets come in many colors.

Like wild parakeets, pet parakeets like living with other parakeets.

The right pet for you?

Parakeets are playful and friendly birds. They enjoy spending time with people. Caring for your pet parakeet is a lot of work, though. You must feed your parakeet and allow it to fly free in your home every day. You will also have to clean your parakeet's cage every week. You will need an adult's help with some of these jobs.

Would you take good care of a parakeet?

Are you ready?

The questions below will help you and your family decide if you are ready for a pet parakeet.

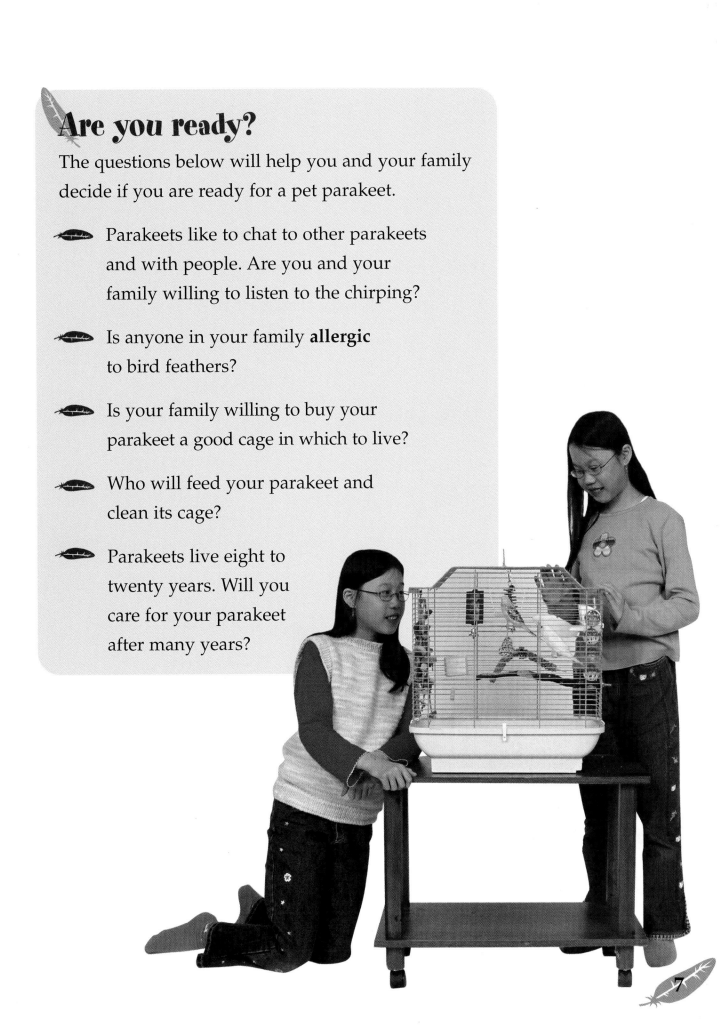

- Parakeets like to chat to other parakeets and with people. Are you and your family willing to listen to the chirping?

- Is anyone in your family **allergic** to bird feathers?

- Is your family willing to buy your parakeet a good cage in which to live?

- Who will feed your parakeet and clean its cage?

- Parakeets live eight to twenty years. Will you care for your parakeet after many years?

So many colors!

There are two types of shell parakeets. One type is the American parakeet. Most of the parakeets in pet stores are American parakeets. The other type of shell parakeet is the English parakeet. English parakeets are **show parakeets**. Show parakeets are entered into contests. You should choose an American parakeet as your pet. American parakeets come in many colors. These pages show a few of the colors.

A cinnamon sky-blue parakeet has white, black, and light-blue feathers.

Albino parakeets are pure white in color.

A yellow parakeet has light yellow feathers with some white feathers around its tail.

The body of an opaline dark-blue parakeet is a rich blue color. Its wings are a mix of black and blue. The feathers on its head are white.

Light green parakeets have green bodies. Their faces are yellow, and their wings are a mix of yellow and black.

Baby parakeets

Baby parakeets are called **chicks**. Chicks **hatch** from eggs laid by their mothers. A female parakeet lays eggs in a **nest box** that attaches to the cage. The box is filled with **bedding**, such as wood shavings. Mother parakeets lay from three to five eggs. The chicks hatch from the eggs in about eighteen days. Newly hatched chicks have no feathers. They cannot see or hear. The mother parakeet feeds and protects them.

A mother parakeet feeds her chicks food from her own mouth.

Growing up

The chicks open their eyes after seven days. It takes four weeks for all their feathers to grow in. The chicks will not leave the nest box for four to five weeks. Once they leave the nest box, they begin to eat on their own. The babies will not be adults until they are a year old!

No unwanted babies!

You do not have to worry that your parakeets will have babies. Parakeets do not **mate** unless you give them a nest box or shredded paper in their cage. Do not give your parakeets a nest box or shredded paper unless you can find good homes for all the chicks.

Picking your parakeet

You can get your pet parakeet from a **breeder** or a pet store. Ask your friends and family if they know of anyone who is giving parakeets away. Make sure you get your parakeet from people who take very good care of animals.

Friends forever

A parakeet likes living with other parakeets. Two male parakeets or a male and a female parakeet will get along well. Do not keep two female parakeets together, though, as they will fight. If you get only one parakeet, you will need to give it a lot of attention to keep it from being lonely.

What to look for

Take your time when you are picking the parakeet you want as your pet. You will probably want the most playful one. Make sure it is also healthy! Ways to tell if it is healthy are listed below.

- A healthy parakeet is active and curious.

- There should be no crust around the parakeet's eyes or beak.

- Check that the parakeet has clean toes and feet.

- The parakeet should not be too thin.

- Make sure the parakeet's feathers lie close to its body.

- The parakeet should be a good, fast flier.

Getting ready

Before you bring your parakeet home, get everything ready for your new pet. These pages show what you will need to care for your parakeet properly.

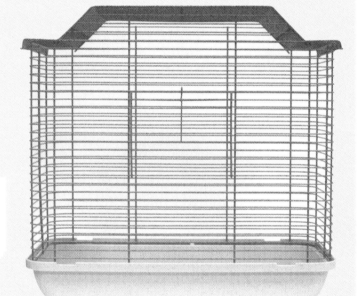

Buy a large cage. The cage should be wide instead of tall.

*Your parakeet will need **wood perches** on which to sit. Make sure your parakeet's toes cannot wrap all the way around the perches.*

*Your parakeet needs a **cuttlebone** to use for sharpening its beak.*

*Put a small cup of **bird sand** into the parakeet's cage every six months.*

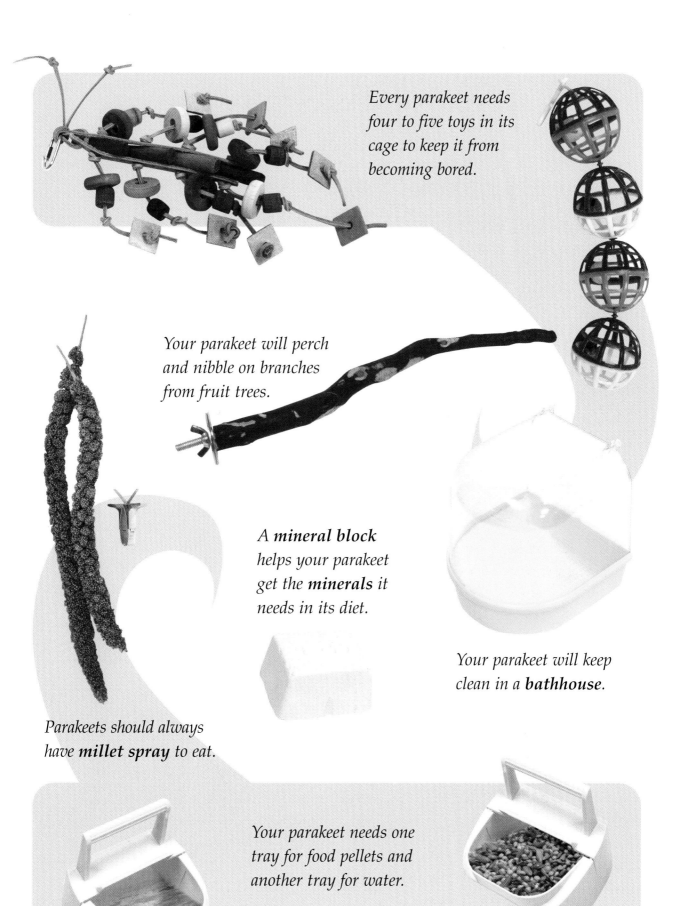

Every parakeet needs four to five toys in its cage to keep it from becoming bored.

Your parakeet will perch and nibble on branches from fruit trees.

A **mineral block** helps your parakeet get the **minerals** it needs in its diet.

Your parakeet will keep clean in a **bathhouse**.

Parakeets should always have **millet spray** to eat.

Your parakeet needs one tray for food pellets and another tray for water.

The bird cage

You can get a cage for your parakeet at a pet store. Ask an adult to help you set it up before bringing your parakeet home. The cage should have metal bars and a plastic base. The base of the cage attaches to the bars with clips. Remember that parakeets are not very big. The spaces between the bars need to be much smaller than your parakeet's body is! Your cage should have a tray that pulls out from the base. This tray will help you keep the cage clean.

mineral block

Your birds will be healthiest in a cage that is at least 30 to 40 inches (76 to 101 cm) long.

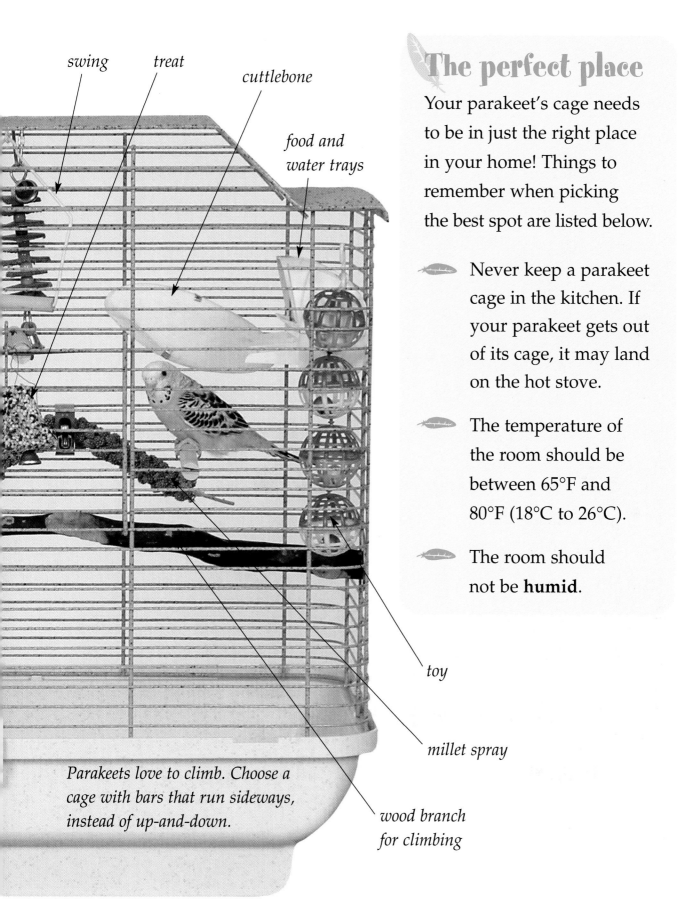

swing

treat

cuttlebone

food and
water trays

toy

millet spray

wood branch
for climbing

*Parakeets love to climb. Choose a
cage with bars that run sideways,
instead of up-and-down.*

The perfect place

Your parakeet's cage needs
to be in just the right place
in your home! Things to
remember when picking
the best spot are listed below.

- Never keep a parakeet
  cage in the kitchen. If
  your parakeet gets out
  of its cage, it may land
  on the hot stove.

- The temperature of
  the room should be
  between 65°F and
  80°F (18°C to 26°C).

- The room should
  not be **humid**.

17

Parakeet food

Parakeets need to eat a variety of foods to stay healthy. You can buy food made just for parakeets at a pet store. Some packaged parakeet foods are mixtures of different seeds, whereas others are mixtures of pellets. Every day, fill your parakeet's dish with pellets, then add only one-quarter of a teaspoon (1.2 ml) of seeds. Choose a seed mixture that has at least eight kinds of seeds. Parakeets also need to eat a variety of fresh fruits and vegetables every day. Your pet will enjoy a small handful of chopped broccoli, carrots, apples, and peas.

For a treat, give your parakeet a stick of seeds glued together with honey. Only give your parakeet a treat once or twice a week, though, or it will gain too much weight!

Fresh water

Make sure your parakeet's water tray is always full of clean, fresh water. Drinking fresh water will keep your parakeet healthy. Don't forget to check the tray for leaks! Thoroughly wash and rinse the tray every day.

Not on the menu

Be very careful when you choose which foods to give your parakeet. Some foods can make your pet very ill!

- Fruits and vegetables that have not been rinsed properly may have harmful **pesticides** on them.

- Never give your parakeet spoiled food. Make sure to take old food out of the cage every day.

- Do not feed your parakeet lettuce, avocado, cabbage, or rhubarb. These foods will make your parakeet sick.

Keeping clean

Parakeets are clean animals. They spend a lot of time **preening**, or cleaning their bodies with their beaks. Your parakeet will still need your help to keep clean, however. These pages show some of the ways to keep your parakeet clean and healthy.

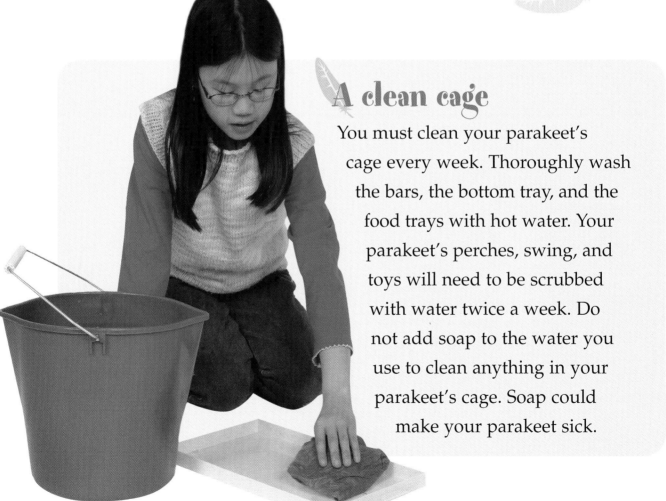

A clean cage

You must clean your parakeet's cage every week. Thoroughly wash the bars, the bottom tray, and the food trays with hot water. Your parakeet's perches, swing, and toys will need to be scrubbed with water twice a week. Do not add soap to the water you use to clean anything in your parakeet's cage. Soap could make your parakeet sick.

Bath time

Most parakeets enjoy taking baths. Buy your parakeet a bathhouse that attaches to the door of its cage. Only add a half inch (1.2 cm) of water to the bathhouse. Make sure the water is not hot. If your parakeet will not take a bath, it might prefer to take a shower! You can shower your parakeet with warm water from a spray bottle. Stop spraying your parakeet if it moves away from the water. Do not worry if your parakeet does not like to get wet. It will keep itself clean.

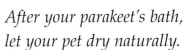

After your parakeet's bath, let your pet dry naturally.

Handle with care

When you bring your parakeet home, give it at least one day alone to explore its cage and to begin to feel at home. You can then train your parakeet to be **handled**, or touched. Always wash your hands before and after handling your parakeet. Follow the steps on these pages to help your pet become used to being handled.

Hand training

Your parakeet needs to become used to you before you can touch it. At the same time every day, fill your hand with some seeds or a treat and move it inside the cage. Hold your hand very still and talk softly to your pet. At first, the parakeet will not come near your hand. After a few days, though, it will begin to trust you.

A gentle touch

When your parakeet is used to your hand, move your finger toward your pet and stroke the front of its body very gently. If your parakeet seems comfortable, gently press on its lower body until it walks onto your finger. Once your pet is on your finger, remove your hand from the cage. The parakeet will probably fly away, so make sure the room is safe. See page 29 to learn some safety tips. As the parakeet flies around, hold your finger in the air to offer it a place to land. Eventually, your parakeet will return to its cage.

Your parakeet might nibble on your skin or hair while it is on your finger or shoulder. Do not worry! It will not hurt you.

Play time

Parakeets are playful and smart. They love climbing, swinging, chewing things, and throwing toys with their beaks. Parakeets need a lot of exercise. To stay healthy, your parakeet should spend a few hours outside its cage every day. When your parakeet is in its cage, make sure there are plenty of fun things for it to do. Playing gives your pet exercise and keeps it healthy.

Your parakeet will use its beak to ring a bell.

Playing on a swing is good exercise!

Parakeets enjoy playing
with toys made of
rope and beads.

Most parakeets enjoy playing
with plastic balls that they can
grab with their beaks.

Sending messages

Did you know that your parakeet can send you messages? Watch how it moves its body. It may be trying to tell you something! Some common ways that parakeets express themselves are shown on these pages.

A parakeet that is too hot will raise its wings slightly away from its body. When your pet does this, move its cage to a cooler room.

An angry parakeet crouches down and opens its beak very wide.

Your parakeet
might clean its
head by rubbing
it against a perch.

A sick parakeet
crouches down on
its perch and fluffs
out all its feathers.

A sleeping parakeet
tucks its head into the
feathers on its back.

Safe parakeets

Your parakeet will not bite you unless you startle it. You can avoid being bitten by not touching your parakeet while it is sleeping. Remember to handle your pet very carefully. Parakeets are easily frightened! If you are bitten by your parakeet, do not push it roughly off your hand. Put your hand inside the bird cage, and your parakeet will hop onto its perch.

Look out!

Before you let your parakeet out of its
cage, look for these possible dangers.

Your parakeet will not
see the glass in a window.
Close the curtains to keep
your parakeet from flying
into a window.

Do not let your parakeet
out of its cage when
someone is cooking food
on the stove. Your parakeet
may burn itself by landing
on the stovetop.

Remove any **poisonous**
plants that your parakeet
may try to eat.

Are there any exposed
electrical cords that
might harm your parakeet
if it bites them?

Do you have any
other pets that might
harm your parakeet?

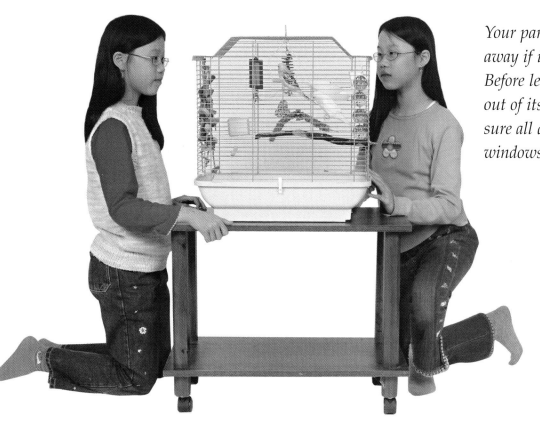

*Your parakeet will fly
away if it gets outdoors.
Before letting your pet
out of its cage, make
sure all doors and
windows are closed.*

Healthy parakeets

A **veterinarian** or "vet" is a medical doctor who treats animals. He or she will help you keep your parakeet healthy. Your parakeet may not let you know it is feeling sick. Take your parakeet to the vet every six months. If you think your parakeet may be sick, take it to the vet right away. The sooner your parakeet is treated by a vet, the better its chances are of staying alive!

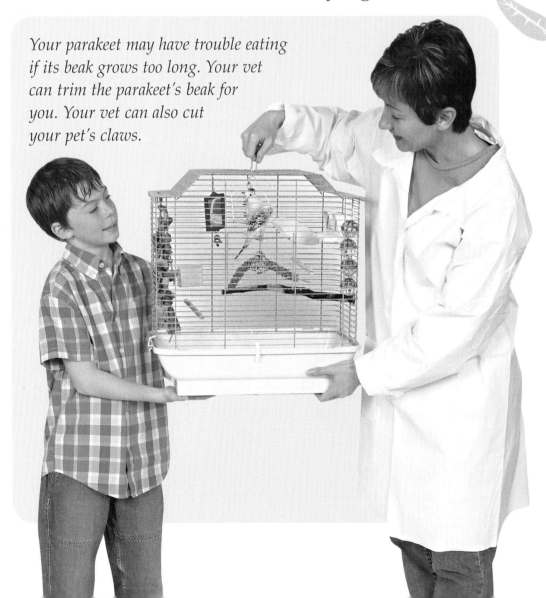

Your parakeet may have trouble eating if its beak grows too long. Your vet can trim the parakeet's beak for you. Your vet can also cut your pet's claws.

When to get help

It is very important to take your parakeet to a vet at the first sign of an illness. Watch for any of the warning signs listed below.

- A sick parakeet may vomit or have trouble breathing.

- Watch for fluids coming out of the parakeet's eyes or nostrils.

- Check for light-colored bumps on the parakeet's legs or feet.

- Make sure the parakeet does not have a wet bottom.

A wonderful life

You need to treat your parakeet with great care. Proper feeding, cleaning, and handling will keep your pet very happy and healthy. A healthy pet parakeet will enjoy a long life. Have fun playing with and caring for your pet, and it will have a great life with you!

Words to know

Note: Boldfaced words that are defined in the book may not appear in the glossary.

allergic Describing someone who has a physical reaction to something

breeder A person who brings budgies together so the budgies can make babies

grassland A large area filled with grasses and trees

hatch To break out of an egg

humid Describing damp air

mate To join together to make babies

minerals Substances, such as salt, that are needed by the body

nest box A box in which female budgies lay eggs

pesticides Chemicals made to kill insects

poisonous Describing something that has substances in it that may harm or kill an animal

Index

1 2 3 4 5 6 7 8 9 0 Printed in the U.S.A. 4 3 2 1 0 9 8 7 6 5